Published by: Experiments in Fiction
Cover Design by: Experiments in Fiction

ISBN-13: 978-1-7394044-7-5

Ingrid Wilson

TO CATCH A POEM

Experiments in Fiction

To Catch a Poem

and other lines I walked

INGRID WILSON

TO MY PARTNER IN RHYME, NICK REEVES

Contents

To Catch a Poem

I came out here today to catch a poem,
like a lepidopterist, swinging her net,
but I've no need to pain those words, or pin them;
just find some lines that you won't soon forget:

Helvellyn's ridge is like your profile, sleeping,
the downy cottongrass, soft like your hair,
the hollow of your collarbone
is mirrored in the ice-carved combe;
though some miles far
I find you everywhere.

I climbed the mountain high to find a poem,
I thought I had a smarter song to sing
than all the meadow pipits, softly chirping
but soon found out I hardly know a thing:

Except, the lonesome wind sighs like your breathing,
except, the sun's a twinkle in your eye,
as if the earth, your form prefiguring
were endless proof of our affinity.

Bannerdale

Never was a green so green
as Bannerdale, that day in June.
I walked along, to find this song:
It is a merry tune!

Never looked the hills so wild
so wisely old, and I, a child
who little knows or cares to know,
by nature's song, beguiled.

Never sang the birds more sweet,
the crickets, chirping at my feet
played nature's mountain symphony
with songs replete.

No, never was a green so green
as Bannerdale, that day in June
one of the pure and fairest sights
I have yet seen.

The Distaff Side

Walking in
Memphis in June
Nubian Queen
sweet oleander
Cleopatra's
Needle weaves a tapestry
throughout the cloth of ages:
strong women
Patti
Carole
Nina
shine bright through these sounds and light
this woven cloth
these printed pages.

Emily
Emily
Charlotte
Billie
with secret thoughts,
desires clothed in Chantilly
Lace, an Orchid in her hair
softens the purple bruise
the silent scream
the unshed tear:

she raises her voice
above the backstreet noise
of hardened minds
who do not care to hear.

There is no darkness without light
nor no light without shadow
in all things, possibility,
from yesterday: tomorrow.

If You Kill the Bird

"You're just an empty cage, girl, if you kill the bird."
– Tori Amos, 'Crucify'

If you kill the bird
you'll rise up every morning
drone-like, yawning
heart un-singing.

If you kill the bird
you'll spend your whole life mourning
yearning, wishing:
unfulfilling.

If you kill the bird
you're dead girl, walking
empty streets through hard
rain falling:

You're just an empty cage girl
void of poetry, unheard,
you're just an empty cage girl
if you kill
you kill the bird.

Child of Our Time

There's a girl who sleeps
under the Earth
who has never yet dared
to draw breath:
she imagines the sky
full of creatures that fly
and the grass decked with flowers
and ferns.

In the bosom of Earth, she is safe:
grounded, firm-fixed
and serene
and she doesn't dare wake
from the wisdom of sleep
where she's curtained and shielded
from pain.

But in that strange sleep dreams do come
to her deep subterranean home
they grow shoots and seek light
though it's never so bright
and with every new dream she's reborn:

She is dreaming a life that her mother remembers,
a life she has never yet known.

Cadralor for Rebirth

I.

Prickles under the skin:
stirring back to life
rebirth, awakening
Alleluia (alleluia)
Amen (amen).

II.

The path, precipitous
is a switchback staircase
its yawning emptiness
instils more awe
than the high crag.

III.

'I lost a lot of blood on the table'
she said, 'I was tabled,'
I said, 'I was scheduled'
I said 'no':
I bleed, I dance.

IV.

Feathers, flowers and silk screens
all those curtain calls
you're all about the light,
the lighting:
I embrace it all.

V.

Mother! I'm coming.
Mother! I'm staying behind.
Your parallel,
your storyteller
whispering the wind.

The Cairns which Mark Our Path

You left in October
walked into the valley
of the shadow of death
and every Autumn since
I skirt the combe's edge.

The dying light speaks to me:
what did you wish to say?
Always seeking refuge
from nightmare's haemorrhage
into the light of day.

Nature's a healer:
kind if you let her
thistle-down whisperer
bracken-fern copperer.

Streams sing remembrances
brook, ghyll, and waterfall
sunset condolences:
silence falls over all.

Watershed

I know the name
of every mountain in these lands
lay my hands on granite rock
and sphagnum moss
spongy lungs of this rich peaty earth
terrain I cross

to walk the wind along the watershed
of Derwent and Eden,
lean into skies, buffeted like a tree
still standing, through a curtain of ice rain
almost to heaven's edge
and back again.

I hug the leeward of Bannerdale Crags
pretend to wend my way back home
yet not so,
for other paths I know
and one half of my wanderer's heart
remains to roam.

Winter's Margin

Shades of the prison house[1]
exist within the shadows
lurk at the peripheries
of winter's margin.

*Our birth is but a sleep
and a forgetting*[2] – what?
The light, from which we came
still burns within.

Cold bites, the penniless poets
strike a match
burn incense, cup wax candles in star-jars
draw closer in.

Your hands recall the sculptor's art
of Michelangelo
and I know all past glories of this earth
await some parallel, hidden rebirth

beyond the edge of time
the porter lifts the northern bar[3]
and spring pours in remembered light
at winter's margin.

The Ballad of Charles Hardin Holley

Charles Hardin Holley
early February
boarded a plane
to spare the journey

overland. He soared above
the earth, to find an early grave,
and leave sweet music in the air,
a wife, to grieve.

Rave on, Buddy Holly, rave —
the airwaves vibrate words of love
into the upper atmosphere:
the hum of turtledoves.

Bewcastle Pilgrimage

This high and lonely landscape
lays no claim to grandeur
only majesty:
magnetic resonances
chime the air, to wake still silent
Cuthbert's bells
to tolling.

The Black Lyne and the White Lyne,
two prongs of a divining rod,
meet north of Roweltown
forming the Lyne, *follow the line,
always the line...*

So I am drawn here,
time and time again,
at threshold moments
life's magnetic compass,
always pointing North.

God bless this sacred wilderness
this wild uncharted openness
these combes and heathered hollows
iron-rich water,
peaty earth.

Ley lines crisscross
this barrenness
like the lines I trace
across your palm with silver
sky—star-marked
as at a lover's birth.

Word Rich, Cash Poor

Word rich, cash poor: some kind of way to live,
don't want that kind of weight pulling me down;
to feel I have a world of wealth to give,
yet possess little I might call my own.

A whisper in the heart blooms on the lips
and greets the air in unforced exhalation,
inspires the hand to flex the fingertips
in *Hallelujah Chorus* exultation.

There is no freedom more than this: creation
— *all other occupations dull the sense* —
do not be limited in expectation,
words' worth affords *abundant recompense*.[4]

For all the world's gold, I'd not change these words:
Let fly! Join morning chorus with the birds.

A Few Pennies...

A few pennies to rub together
berries, for the coming winter
bottled, labelled
placed upon a shelf

like preserved cherries,
pears or quinces
compassed, weighed:
a measured year of dearth[5]

as at a birth, or Coronation,
profit margins, revelation:
What we lack?
The will to save ourselves.

In pedalling the petalled road
I shoulder my weight of the load
put my foot down:
Release it to the sky.

Mardale Blue

From Mardale Green
to Mardale Blue
gaggle, goose
crow, cuckoo:

they're singing in the village choir
sound drowned before you

came, Surveyor,
Corporation
handshake, Mayor
all corruption

dried out lake shows your mistake:
unchecked consumption

from Measand School
to the Dun Bull
echoes left
of voices, cool

whispers, on the lake-bed lie
deep, blue and mournful.

Sigh, Sough, Bend Low

Sigh, sough, bend low,
sing a song of sorrow:
I hold your branch
and feel the wrench
of what may come tomorrow.

Reach high, shield eye
join hands above me:
your branches bare
in bud this year
and ever after? Maybe.

I yearn, will learn
to spring forth like bracken
underfoot,
like peat, like soot
I pray to green, not blacken.

Regenesis Cadralor

I.

April evening
the lake a pure blue sheet
a red boat moored and edged in ochre
songbirds chatter
golden, light.

II.

Acapella dreaming, you
tapping on the kitchen floor
reel-to-reel
cut to a scene
of smoke, wraiths, dancing.

III.

Genesis imagined
stars burst into
rivers of white light
faint as whisper,
hard as heartbeat.

IV.

A shipwreck
on a storm-tossed sea
through centuries
rusts in the bay
out past the tide wrack.

V.

East of Eden
Pennines rise
like sleeping megafauna
remnants of a lost ice age
we wake, imagining.

Tolling Bells

And all we hear are tolling bells
telling fortunes, wishing wells
well-wishers washed in pools of tears
all eyes and ears
all eyes and ears

Are turned towards the funeral
the heart has had its coronal[6]
as silence ends the reign of years
the sky rains tears
the sky rains tears

We listen at the close of day
for birdsong, as a lullaby
returns us to our mother earth
as at our birth
as at our birth

And we, when once that song is done
where wandering souls are welcomed home
hoping to see the stars at night
put out the light
put out the light

We Crown the Wrong Things King

Money, power, wealth and status:
we crown the wrong things King.
Simple laughter, human kindness
past considering.

Gas-guzzling cars, communities
gated, to shut out love:
we crown the wrong things king, we say,
"Ordained by God above."

The things we do best, with our hearts;
our art, our joy, our song
devalued, shunned, not set apart:
we crown the wrong things King.

So, on this coronation day,
should you be listening
beyond the pageantry, I say,
"We crown the wrong things, King."

Where only Love Exists

There is a place where only love exists,
beneath the magic of your fingertips,
till all I feel is unencumbered joy,
a wide-eyed pilgrim, I
seek succour here
where only love exists.

In the mossy clefts of a steep-sided valley
through undergrowth, to overarching sky
where larks ascend
and ravens wend
their ragged-wingéd way
here in this place where only love exists.

On the high path towards a low fell summit
in the blue sparkle of your loving eye
at eventide,
through morning's aching beauty
let me stay
in hope to play
where only love exists.

In Durham

The curtains are parted,
the geese honk their horns
slung under the moon in Durham;

they wade in the Wear
the day after the storm
beneath the half-moon in Durham.

Sweet memories soar
in my heart, ever-warm
just watching the moon in Durham

and I hold you so dear
near my breast, in my arms
as a new day dawns in Durham.

Born Aloft

Borne aloft
with our first gulp of air
we suck in sight, as sound assaults our ears.

Borne aloft
this burden, worn with care,
for all earth's woes, shed through the Vale of Tears.

Born aloft
with angel-voices singing
couched in love, all warm within the womb.

Born aloft
above tortured hands, wringing
blood out of the earth, to court our doom.

Bourn, a loft —
a bounteous land becoming
refuge in a time of want and need.

Bourn, a loft,
candle-lit, welcoming
your love, a balm to cancel cold and greed.

You - A Sonnet

A summer field on a heatwave day;
a lake of frosted mirror glass in winter;
a cuckoo call late in the month of May:
my once upon a time, my ever after.

A breath of outdoor air when walls cave in;
a blossom bower, a Sunday afternoon;
a bed of bluebell flowers bordered in green;
a peony, as May bursts into June.

A walk along the beach in late July;
an August promenade beside the lake;
the light which dwells in every lover's eyes—
deep honeyed drink, the lover's thirst to slake:

All of these things and more, you are to me
unfolding, golden, mirrored ecstasy.

The Hedgerow

The robin is our go-between, and
swallow, magpie, sparrow, wren
know our desires, discern our wants:
the hedgerow flowers, our confidantes

grow cautiously towards the sun
with half a bud-ear tuned upon
sweet, whispered words that lovers speak
alone, where no-one else may seek

to disturb all their loving chatter
nor dare to ask, 'What is the matter?'
No matter what the world may do
beneath this hedgerow, I'll love you.

A Garden, full of Birdsong

A garden, full of birdsong, bathes my mind,
levelling out the aches, and furrowed creases;
the iron grasp of winter lies behind,
as daffodils light up the children's faces.

The meadowlark and sparrow greet the day
while swallows on the wing, returning, flourish:
The song thrush and the gentle-footed jay
make busy at their nests, their young to nourish.

Lapwings, in their curious flight, scour wheatfields
searching for flies and moths to feed their chicks,
while on the beach,
from Cullercoats to North Shields,
gulls and starlings plunder human picnics:

Here, you and I make merry in our nest,
King of the East, and Queen of the Wild West.

Just Gentle Rain

June light spills in through the window, so silently;
seagulls carouse in the gutters with gallantry;
no other sound filters down through our reverie:
Just gentle rain,
just gentle rain
and your loving me.

Bedclothes are tossed to the ground
—fall as if on cue,
other clothes, stripped
like the bough of an ancient yew
bent into arrows
whose flight follows softly through
just, gentle rain,
just gentle rain
and my loving you.

Another layer gone, and we edge in on ecstasy:
bodies entwined into time, and with sanctity
sound echoes sound and reverberates, endlessly
just, gentle rain,
this gentle reign
of your loving me.

Starling Companion

Starling companions crowd the picnic table
pied wagtail hops along his waggle-dance
seagulls strut, searching for scraps of chips
beside the bench:
it's spring,
and all the earth is clothed in joy.

Two magpies' courtship heralds balmy summer
unfolding with the turning of the year
while April winds blow blossoms:
gently falling, petalled rainfall
whispering, still,
for all the world to hear.

All These Signs of Spring

Trees burst into blossom
and birds dance on the wing
as happiness forgotten comes
with all these signs of spring.

I ride out under billowed skies
welcome the sun, rising
while April rains wash winter pains
away, at signs of spring.

Forget-me-nots and daisies
brighten all the hedgerow's length:
with all these signs of spring return
renewed, my hope and strength.

How Quickly and how Slowly Pass the Years

How quickly and how slowly pass the years:
the surf, rolling, roars in, the surge sucks sand
receding, washed with tidal waves and tears.

The children wait for summer; winter's thaw
that seemed to take forever, melts the land.
How slowly, yet how quickly pass the years.

Two bodies grown together, loving, dear
walk out into the sunset, hand in hand
receding, washed with tidal waves and tears.

A lifetime's striving, turmoil, hopes and fears
against time's compass falter, fail to stand:
how quickly, yet how slowly roll the years

Till, through time's mists, a golden road appears,
building a bridge from sea to shining strand
receding, washed with tidal waves and tears.

Surrender sorrow's burden, earthly cares:
life's path, though laden, lightens in the end
receding, washed with tidal waves and tears
how slowly, yet how quickly pass the years.

I Look out to Sea

And I look out to sea, to see
the things eye cannot see;
to hear the howl of wind behind
the ear's eternity.

And I look out beyond the dawn
where daylight, undergone
begins its creep around the earth
birthed by the setting sun.

I look out on the firmament
of frenzied human strife;
and pause, breathe in the merriment
loosed from the bonds of life.

A Galloway Ballad

The pasture so green
beneath skies richly grey...
The pull of Galloway, my love,
the pull of Galloway.

The razor-edge cliffs
where the land falls away...
The lull of Galloway, my love,
the lull of Galloway.

The shipwreck below
'neath the rocks, rusts away...
The hull of Galloway, my love
the hull of Galloway.

While we walk hand in hand
where time's grip holds no sway...
The Mull of Galloway, my love
The Mull of Galloway.

Hartsop

Hartsop
where lovers' hearts hop
heading down the valley at the close of day

Ghyllside or hillside
over the mountain-top
happily, wearily, wending their way.

Heart's leap
at golden light's last lap
over the autumn sky, dying away.

Hearts stop
true enough, all hearts stop:
what better place than Hartsop at the close of day?

Crossing and Recrossing the Tyne

Crossing and recrossing the Tyne
in winter, under gentle rain
beneath the lees
these windblown trees
lean close, pull one another in...

Through softened sunlight in springtime
as Easter brings rebirth, we sing
a song of joy,
just you and I
crossing and recrossing the Tyne.

Through waves of heat as summer's spine
arches, and the rolling main
laps up the shore
I do adore
crossing and recrossing the Tyne.

Where autumn weaves its magic line
through leaves which fall in tune with time
like gentle rain
my love remains
crossing and recrossing the Tyne.

Publication Credits

'The Distaff Side' first published in Issue X of Free Verse Revolution (July 2023)

'Regenesis Cadralor' first published in Gleam — Journal of the Cadralor (Issue 6, June 2023)

Endnotes

1   From Wordsworth, 'Ode: Intimations of Immortality from Recollections of Early Childhood'

2   *Ibid.*

3   Adapted from Blake, *Book of Thel*

4   'Abundant recompense,' from Wordsworth's 'Lines Composed a Few Miles above Tintern Abbey, On Revisiting the Banks of the Wye during a Tour. July 13, 1798'

5   Allusion to Blake, 'Proverbs of Hell'

6   Allusion to Wordsworth, 'Ode: Intimations of Immortality from Recollections of Early Childhood'

Further EIF Poetry Titles

Archery in the UK
by Nick Reeves and Ingrid Wilson
ISBN: 9781739757786

Inspired by the *Lyrical Ballads* of Wordsworth and Coleridge, two authors set out to pen a contemporary homage to this timeless collection. As the collaboration progresses, however, the poetry and the unique narrative it carries takes on a life of its own. Thus, the authors come to tell their story through a collection of ballads, sonnets, pantoums and other forms.

40 Poems At 40
by Ingrid Wilson
ISBN: 9781739757700

40 Poems is the debut poetry collection from Ingrid Wilson. It is poetry of place and space, and here lie the clues and the beauty to Wilson's poetry. Her work is charted, landscaped, travelled, explorative and laden with adventure.

Three-Penny Memories, A Poetic Memoir
by Barbara Harris Leonhard
ISBN: 9781739757762

"Do you love your mother?" This provocative question provides the catalyst for this stunning poetic memoir from Pushcart Nominee Barbara Harris Leonhard, who considers where her loyalties lie following her mother's diagnosis with Alzheimer's.

All Grown Up Now
by Kim M. Russell
ISBN: 9781739404437

This collection shows what it was like to grow up in a family in the decades after the war, how it shapes the individual, what they learn and keep in their heart, the rituals and routines that are handed down the generations.

In The Shadow of Rainbows
by Selma Martin
ISBN: 9781739404444

In this dazzling debut poetry collection, author Selma Martin points the way to the beauty in the everyday, the shadow of the rainbow, and the silver lining at the edge of every cloud.

Milton Keynes UK
Ingram Content Group UK Ltd.
UKHW020640041223
433752UK00017B/828